Loose Leaves AND Acorn Bits

A Collection of Fall Poems

C.W. PEN

Loose Leaves and Acorn Bits

By C.W. Pen

Published by Kevin E. Winters, 12700 Denny Court, Upper Marlboro MD, International Standard Book Number:
978-0-9977334-8-8

Printed in the United States of America

Page layout by Artiest Design and Illustration

Dedication

To my awesome family, thank you for your support
and encouragement. I love you!

TABLE OF CONTENTS

Fall

The apples look like fall.
The apples taste like fall.

The weather feels like fall.
The weather smells like fall.

The leaves sound like fall.
So I check the wall.
September 22nd
Yep! The calendar says it's fall!

The Malicious Side of Fall

The season of seasons
Has a dark side.
The temperature drops
From 80 to 35.

For mammals,
They have their fur and hide.
While humans have it easy
As they simply go inside.
The insects see this and try to do the same.
Some crawl in from cracks,
Others through the drain.

They then make their homes
And travel around.
Spiders in their webs
And crickets under the bed.
Protected and collected,
Feeling snug,
Until someone yells out the word "Bug!"

Then splat! The insect goes with all of its juices!
Running is useless for humans are ruthless.
Except for the ones that take them outside
Only for the cold to kill them
Freezing their insides.

So bye-bye to the spiders, mosquitos, and butterflies.
It took me some time, but now I realize.
Fall is a killer with golden-orange eyes.

Orange Tinted Autumn

Absolute silence,
Except for the rustle of trees.
The red autumn breeze pushes the pool of leaves
Across the green grass and pine cones
To be put in a pile to jump in.

Then once the jumping is done,
The adults come out and have their fun.
With their rakes and bags,
The hours pass as the leaves disappear.
Sure the leaves go, but the feeling never does.
This feeling of warmth and cold.
Where the orange-tinted Autumn
Switches from orange to gold.

The Month of September

The beginning of fall
Starts in the month of September.
Quite the chilling season
But quite the time to remember
Of everything you forgot
Over the course of the summer
For school starts back up which is quite the bummer.

You might not be excited
But your socks and coats are.
Ready to be worn to keep you warm
Prepping you for the season,
And it's quite impossible to be sad at this time of year
For fall doesn't give you a reason.

There are festivals and holidays
Full of warmth and culture.
Apples that taste even sweeter by color.
All of these happen later
In October and November,
And you can experience them.
That's if you survive the cold of September.

Acorn Rain

Sharp, hard rain
Falls from the sky
With light brown shells and acorn tops.

And while some crash to the ground,
Cracking and breaking,
Others land in the autumn grass
Where the debris is sent in all directions
Never having any real intention.

And not to mention the animals that collect them.
To gobble up and feast on
To survive the next season.

Loose Leaves and Acorn Bits

Littered loose leaves
And bits of acorn
Remain on the floor for days and days.

The constant crunch of their bodies
Should only be enjoyed outside,
And their remains should be swept away.

But if they're found inside,
Take a broom and sweep them into a pile,
Then open the door,
As the autumn wind sends them elsewhere.

Where?
Who knows.
And honestly, who cares.
As long as the home of me, leaves, and acorns are never shared.

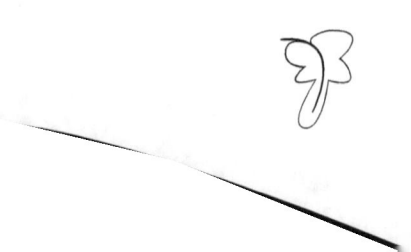

Dancing Leaves

Pirouetting leaves
Elegantly swaying
With no needed training
As they keep in formation.

The lighting was perfect
As they spot turned left.

Each one looked angelic
As each then spun to the right.

Next was their landing
Which needed to be precise.
But they're professionals at this
Knowing each other's shape and size.

The wind knew which way to swing them,
How to gently weave them,
Knowing how to catch its breath
And when to breathe again.

Then they somewhat splashed
Not thrashing to the ground.
Some flip when they landed
Landing right where they anticipated.

Honestly, we take leaves for granted.
They give us a show, and I'm the only one chanting.
The only one asking for an encore
Cause it was truly amazing.

Clear Car Thoughts

I'm sitting in the car
While my dad drives,
And without my phone,
I realize what passes me by.

Blue and greenhouses
With decorator fountains.
Giant trees with colorful fruit.
Huge stones and clouds, but no mountains in view.
I wished we would see a mountain or two.

Harvested cornfields
With old looking barns,
And the barn's workers who look even older.
Two bulls rubbing shoulders with a drone flying over
As the fall season gets even colder.

Blue water with a blue sky to match.
People of all colors hugging as we pass.
Along with small shops that boost the economy
As we drive by happily sightseeing.

Hideaway Hands

Autumn's cold isn't so terrible.
You can prepare so it can be bearable.
And it feels somewhat magical
To every part of my body that's not my hands.

They shiver, and they shake
As the frost nibbles at their nerves.
And not knowing how much more they can take,
They hide in their homes at the side of my pants.
"Shuffle Shuffle" is all I hear
As they burrow by everything I keep most dear
Until they reach the very bottom.

There, they gather as much heat as they can
In the formation of a warm, heat-absorbing fist.
But sometimes my hands get a little too warm
As if they have their own little fireplaces and heated mattresses.
But little do they know they'll have to come out soon
Cause I use my hands for almost everything I do.

Pants Size

I don't know my pants size.
Should I?
How would I?
Is it important?

If I find it, what will it be?
Will it be too big for me?
Will it be too small?
Does it change like the seasons
Like summer turning to fall?
How'd I go my whole life without knowing at all?

The Month of October

How does school feel?
What's the deal?
Are you dreaming?
Is this real?
Cause fall looks very different than before.

Tons of red and a whole lot more yellow covers the front yard's lawn.
The golden strike of the sun is quite harsh,
But it's most beautiful at dawn.
The apples are juicy
And nobodies moody
Except for those who hate the cold.
The wind carries this cold downtown and pass the mountains,
And then carried even further elsewhere
So someone else can feel the shaking shiver it brings.
Then the night is filled with creatures and frights,
Halloween decorations and artificial lights
Shine brightly making the night seem less nightly

It's Autumn at its loveliest.
Autumn at it's healthiest.
Living and breathing as if it were human.
With its cold weather and fun nature giving most people grins
And about the only time we humans get where the Earth seems free of
sin.

Sweet Potato Pie

Pumpkin Pie is something I've never had
But I had an apple pie from McDonald's.
And blackberry pie sounds gross.
So I'll have to rely on my trusty sweet potato pie.

Sweet and salty with a rusty color,
Made only from the sweetest potatoes and butter
With a crunchy crust that's amazing and delicious,
Sweet potato pie is definitely a must.

Autumn Scented Candles

The smell of pumpkin spice
Resonates from the hallway.
Along with a small ember flickering on a wick
Which burns the candle's smell away.
Slowly but surely
For what feels like an eternity.

And once the candle has died,
No longer producing its sweet scent of autumn,
Another candle is brought to replace it,
And let's face it,
Apple pie smells better than pumpkin spice.
Its color is nice, but apple pie's is nicer.
Pumpkins are bitter while apples are sweeter.

It's a nice little change.
A great change of pace.
I happily walk by sniffing
As the candle does the race.
Burning and burning for hours upon end.
The flame sits there wavering, still taking in oxygen.

But then goes my apple pie candle
And with it goes the cozy feeling it gave me,
My constant hunger and apple pie craving.
And I find it honestly amazing,
How uplifting candles can be.
They're quite dangerous, yes,
But who knew danger could smell so sweet.

Cinnamon Covered Treats

Cinnamon covered treats
Become too spicy to eat
If there's too much cinnamon!
It will make your mouth feel warm and dry
And cause you to yelp and cry!
Water can help as it washes this burning sensation goodbye
But at this time of year, it's in everything!
Cakes and shakes,
Goods that are cooked or baked,
Even gummies and taffy,
And apples and pears and almost everything healthy!
So if you don't want to feel your mouth melting,
Bring a bottle of water everywhere!

Halloween!

Halloween is considered quite the special day
And the kids wish it could last for an eternity
But for me, it's different
Life will move on rather quickly for my family.

We're top tier Christians
Paying no mind to "The Devil's Day"
Well, that's what they call it
To me, it's just a silly holiday

A bunch of bright lights,
Cool and creative costumes
As the night's filled with laughter
And it's sky with a bright shining moon.
But looking and listening is all I can do
Watching and hearing the kids knock on our door
Only for no answer
Which they remember
And now know not to come to this house ever.

So every year, I light a candle and eat salted pumpkin seeds
They're a lot healthier than candy
Not very filling
But rather tasty
And I never have to worry about them being stolen or my safety
Like the very few adults who check their kid's candy
For any cruel, sick trickery that Halloween brings.

The Month of November

Oh, I remember
A time where Autumn had a distinct color in it's leaves
Now they're brown and white.

Oh, I remember
A time when there were frights in the streets
And the light of the moon would mix with the Earth neatly.

A time where acorns and pine cones crunched,
Now they sit there in pieces
Making no more than a mush.

We still have Thanksgiving, which I'm thankful for
There'll be tons of food, family, and more
But without Autumn's beauty, what will become of it?

It will be a bird with no soar,
A dresser with no drawers,
A no shining Sun, a simple season with no fun.

What has happened to Autumn?
I heard multiple times "The Season's Changing," and I gotta stay tough
But this whole changing cycle that I'm witnessing is ruff

Oh, I remember the cold nights of September
And the color of October
And witnessed the death of Autumn in November.

Oh, how could I forget.
The killer was Winter.
But then again, why would I want to remember.

Magnesium Sky

Gloomy
But beautiful
With roars of thunder
While still peaceful.
A grey veil that shields out outer space
And let's loose lightning and gentle rain upon the Earth
Giving it moisture
And keeping everything here alive
Oh, what would we do without a heavy magnesium sky?

Turkey

I wonder how the turkey feels
Cooked up, spiced up, served up
On a silver platter
For all of us to gobble up.

He's not alone though
To his left is cheesy macaroni
To his right is his old friend, now ham.
Above him arrives the gravy boat.
And below, his was feathered friend Sam.

And as he looks around the table,
Around the corn and cranberry sauce,
They're people with closed eyes holding hands
Praying a thankful prayer.

The Death of Autumn Pt. I

The amber-colored season
Has had a good long run.
Three tremendous months to be exact,
In fact,
People still look back to the fat turkey they ate
Along with the other edible items on their plate,
But then you can start to notice.

You can start to notice it's signs,
The current state of Autumn,
My favorite season and the skys above
Showed some scary things that consisted of:

Naked oak trees looking over its dead withered leaves.
The absence of geese and a terrible cold breeze.
The smashing of pumpkins in the backyards of many
Only for the seeds to be eaten by birds, if any.

Many of the ornaments are gone,
To the ghosts in the yard, to the ghouls on the roof.
And the sky is colder, white, and dead-looking
With a diamond colored Sun instead of a golden one.

So this is it
The "Changing of Seasons" phrase was made by a demon.
A demon who knew what has happened from the beginning.
My eyes have been opened, and now I can see it clearly
As Winter slowly kills fall and gracefully hides the body.

The Death of Autumn Pt 2

Winter is here
And it wants you to know
It's the next season, the best season
And prepare for snow.
But what happened to fall
Where did it go?
As I step outside, I already know.

The white flurry falls quickly,
Rapidly but gently,
And every step I take feels extra crunchy.
It's not just the ice crystals under my feet
But bits of acorns and hidden leaves.

So I kicked the snow, and there they were, (and under my feet)
Little bits of acorns and orange shivering leaves.
How long they were trapped
I had no idea in mind,
But for the short time I ran for help, they were covered by white in no
time.

I continued my walk through the harsh Winter's cold.
I remember September's along with its glow of gold
Or was it orange and green?
Or black or brown?
I can't recall with all this white around.

Halloween has passed and the festivals are over,
No more pirouetting leaves nor four-leaf clovers,
Instead, there's Christmas that overflows with color
Along with children up late
Trying to see the Santa Clause wonder.

Winter stole everything fall had
The snacks, the colors,
Increasing the joy of the people
At the same time, killing Autumn
And hiding the body so no one would see it.

And as Autumn's cold corpse starts to rot away,
For a good long time,
About 90 days,
Spring will kill Winter and take it's place.
Then, Summer will pick the petals of Spring.

And eventually, real soon
Autumn will rise again,
Killing Summer, its heat, bugs and then,
Shine its golden-orange eyes upon them.

C.W. Pen

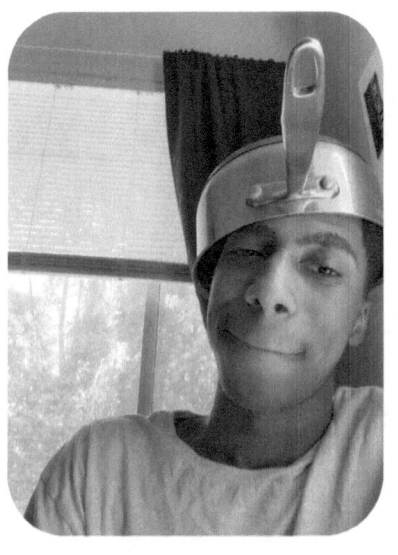

C.W. Pen is a fantastic storyteller whose mind swirls with exciting tales. His captivating writings, always brewing with mystery, inspires readers of all ages to enjoy a temporary journey into the fantastical worlds and creative narratives that seep through the tip of his pen. Whether crafted as narrative or poetry, each word reflects his passion for words and his willingness to share his creativity with the world.

He is sixteen years old and is an eleventh-grade high schooler. He is also a passionate photographer and currently utilizes that talent to capture his high school band's treasured moments. He lives in Maryland with his parents and three siblings.